The Last Text Message

by

Various Artists

First published 2025 by The Hedgehog Poetry Press

Published in the UK by
The Hedgehog Poetry Press
Coppack House, 5
Churchill Avenue
Clevedon
BS21 6QW

www.hedgehogpress.co.uk

Copyright © The Hedgehog Poetry Press 2025

The right of individual contributors to be identified as the author of their work has been asserted in accordance with the Copyright, Designs and Patents Act 1988.

All rights reserved. No part of this publication may be reproduced, stored in or introduced into a retrieval system, or transmitted in any form, or by any means (electronic, mechanical, photocopying, recording or otherwise) without prior written permissions of the publisher. Any person who does any unauthorised act in relation to this publication may be liable for criminal prosecution and civil claims for damages,

9 8 7 6 5 4 3 2 1

A CIP Catalogue record for this book is available from the British Library.

ISBN: 978-1-916830-52-3

Contents

Gerald Killingworth 5

Amanda Hill 6

Julie De Brito 7

Liz Kendall 8

Nigel Kent 9

Roger Waldron 10

Wendy Goulstone 11

Christopher House 12

Philippa Ramsden 13

Julie Leoni 14

Miriam Moore 15

Patricia M Osborne 16

Phil Santus 18

Neil Windsor 19

GERALD KILLINGWORTH

Epitaph

The poetry
is our deathbed confessions,
form sacrificed
in the urgent need
to tell people clearly
how much we love them.

So much to put on paper
when an Art
a World
and Ourselves
are dying.

AMANDA HILL

The Final Text Message

For I have lived a thousand lives in one
And died a thousand deaths
The time to leave come upon me fast
I must go and breathe my very last
Each day here has been sublime
Revel as I allay the Laws of Time

JULIE DE BRITO

Last Text and Testament

My last wishes for u
after all u did 2 me

Ur always 30 secs late for trains
and ur carriage smells of drains

U don't see the milk has curdled
until u sip ur tea and
ur porch light goes out
before u find ur key

LIZ KENDALL

Salvage

No grave, no stone, no fuss.
Use me up: every scrap for science or
cut my skin into ribbons and dance me round a maypole.
I don't care, I'll be dead.
But dance.

NIGEL KENT

Too late

From the time
I was born
I ran and
ran uphill
not daring
to look back
till at last
my lungs gave
out to find
there never
was a race
or a chase
though I'd still

lost.

ROGER WALDRON

Let's Fly Like Kite

your last text said I was your Dick
Van Dyke to your Julie Andrews
and you're on top of John Lewis
ready to dive into Barkers Pool
make a clean sweep without
any strings attached

WENDY GOULSTONE

My Darling Dove
my one regret
is that
I did not say
I love you
that last day
as you lay in bed
waiting
for the operation
so I say it now
my darling
I lo ve you
I love you
I love you
XXX

CHRISTOPHER HOUSE

One last text

I drive along this back street texting
Too absorbed to hit the brake
A child's run out in front and next thing
I'm attending my own wake

PHILIPPA RAMSDEN

Lest I Forget

Please slip these
into my willow casket
when no one is looking:

pen, favourite notebook
radio to listen to shipping forecast
bus pass
snowdrop and bluebell bulbs

And shush, don't tell a soul.

JULIE LEONI

Burn me hot over fallen branches
Inhale me
Crush my bones

Smell me
on your
Fingers

Spread me
Wide

To
Worms

- Wait -

As
I
Re
Form

Slippery
Ripe
Plump
Dripping

Suck
Swallow

Bite
Into
Me
Once more

MIRIAM MOORE

I'm sorry. Please, don't cry
It isn't you – it's me, you see
You'll just ask why
And wonder if you missed a sign, a clue
To what I was about to do
There wasn't. We were just actors
Who ran out of characte

PATRICIA M OSBORNE

Last Words

Soak up the love,
saturate your sponge
with special moments,
savour the memories,
don't let them trickle away.

I leave to you...

I leave to you a chance to retreat
in my fictional stories and poems

I leave to you my thousands of words
immerse your mind and escape in my books

PHIL SANTUS

Goodbye

So, do not weep for me, my friend.
I had my time, and it was good.
I lived my life within this world,
the world we've still not understood.

I know a place where water breaks
upon the edge of sacred bays,
where evidence of life remains,
that thrived within more ancient days.

Ah, life with all your mystery,
I held you close upon my breast,
I reasoned, sought and nurtured you,
as if you'd been my valued guest.

NEIL WINDSOR

Finale

This is it
A final throw of the dice
With wolves at the door
I'm paying the ultimate price
For a life of raging excess
Causing upset and deep distress
We reap what we sow
So now at last, it's time to go